W9-CDA-971

1/2014

Hampshire County Public Library
153 West Main Street
Romney, WV 26757

ANIMALS
AT WORK

ANIMALS
IN THE
MILITARY

Alexis Burling

Enslow Publishing
101 W. 23rd Street
Suite 240
New York, NY 10011
USA

enslow.com

checkpoints Places where people or cars are searched by an authority figure (such as a police officer) before being allowed to continue.

detect To find or discover the presence of something.

echolocation The use of sound waves and echoes to figure out where an object is in a certain area.

hostage A person who is captured by someone else and held, usually for money.

mascot A person or animal used as a symbol to represent a group and bring good luck.

navigate To figure out a way to get to a place using directions or maps.

patrol The act of walking or riding around an area to make sure it is safe.

snipers People who shoot at other people from a hidden place.

sonar A way to find things underwater using sound waves.

veteran Someone who fought in a war or served in the military as a soldier or sailor.

CONTENTS

Introduction

It was October 1942. World War II was raging across Europe. A new army soldier went to his captain's tent to ask about his orders. He was in for a big surprise. There was a giant Syrian brown bear plopped in front of the tent. The bear's name was Wojtek.

Wojtek served with Polish troops after he was found in the mountains of Iran as a bear cub. They fed him

Who (or What) Used All the Water?

Legend has it that Wojtek taught himself how to use faucets. One time, it was so hot that he snuck into the bathing area and turned on all the showers. He used up a month's water supply in one day!

Brown bears do not normally serve in the military. But Wojtek's job made him famous!

milk and sometimes beer out of a bottle. Wojtek liked to wrestle and play soccer with the soldiers. He showered with them, too.

The troops loved the six-foot-tall (1.8-meter-tall) bear. He made them feel happy and forget about fighting. Sometimes he helped out by carrying heavy loads to and from battle.

"For people who are far from families, far from their home country…[having Wojtek around] was very important," one soldier told *BBC News*.

When World War II ended in 1945, Wojtek was sent to a farm in Scotland with other Polish soldiers. Later he was moved to the Edinburgh Zoo.

Fact

The Syrian bear, one of sixteen types of brown bear worldwide, lives in mountain ranges across the Middle East.

"He was very much a part of the community and attended dances, concerts, local children's parties," the farm's owner told *TIME* magazine.

In this book, you will meet other animal mascots like Wojtek. You will also be introduced to bomb-sniffing dogs, dolphins

Dogs are one of the most commonly used animals in the military.

that find lost objects in the ocean, and cats that spy for the government. These amazing animals continue to shape the course of military history. Woof! Woof! It's time to send in the troops!

Tough
Transporters

Bears like Wojtek are not common in the military. Most brown bears do not like to be around people. But lots of other huge animals have served in armies all over the world. Why? Because of their size.

In ancient times, elephants were often used on the battlefield. During the Roman Empire, they stood in a line down the center of a charging army. Because of their

Squeal!

Pigs are smart. They also run fast and make a lot of noise. During the Roman Empire, pigs were used as weapons. Why? Elephants are terrified of pigs. One army would block another army's advances by setting dozens of pigs loose on the battlefield. The elephants stopped in their tracks!

Elephants are massive creatures. Their big bodies can stop an advancing army!

In the US Civil War (1861 to 1865), horses were often used in battle.

thick skin and sharp tusks, the elephants rarely got hurt. Their swinging trunks could also knock down lots of enemy soldiers at once.

In other areas of the world, such as in India, Russia, and South Asia, elephants were used to carry supplies. Before helicopters and tanks, they carried troops into the countryside. Their big feet easily stomped over mountains, through rivers, and across rocky land.

During the Revolutionary War between the United States and Great Britain, both armies rode horses into battle. In the 1600s and 1700s, Native American tribes used horses when fighting, too. These beautiful animals could gallop, run, and quickly change direction. Other animals used in the United States and other countries for transportation or to carry around heavy military supplies are mules, llamas, oxen, camels, and even donkeys!

Fact
Over sixteen million animals served in the military during World War II and were used for transport, communication, and companionship.

Digging
Detectors

Like horses, dogs have had jobs in the military for more than two thousand years. Dogs have a special skill that helps them do their work perfectly. They have an excellent sense of smell.

Because of their sensitive snouts, military dogs are used for many purposes. Patrol dogs ride with the troops on their missions. Scout dogs help detect snipers, who shoot from hiding spots and can be hard to see, and other enemies in a patrol area. Search-and-rescue dogs look for lost people or objects.

Fact
According to the US War Dogs Association, dogs have saved more than ten thousand lives throughout US history.

This dog is being trained to detect different scents in his environment.

A baby rat learns how to sniff out dangerous land mines.

Bzzzz! Bombs!

Honeybees are kept in glass tubes at dangerous military checkpoints. If a person carrying explosives tries to get through, the bees will buzz around the tube until the person is caught.

Mine-detection dogs are trained to sniff out buried explosives. Mines are small bombs that can hurt a lot of people.

But dogs are not the only super sniffers in the military. Believe it or not, rats are used, too! These pesky rodents have terrible vision, especially at night. But their tiny noses can pick up smells human noses can't. Plus, the critters are small. They can scurry into areas that are too dangerous for people and dogs. One rat can search over two thousand square feet (two hundred square meters) in twenty minutes!

Perhaps the most surprising animal used in the military is the honeybee. Like dogs, these insects track explosive devices. Bees love sugar. They are trained to

Honeybees use their antennae to pick the scent of bomb ingredients out of the air.

associate sugar water with TNT, a material used in bombs. When checking for bombs in an area, soldiers release a swarm of honeybees. Then they track where the honeybees go. If the bees dive toward a spot, there is probably a bomb there.

Sneaky Spies

If you have a sister or brother, you probably know what spying is. You sneak into each other's rooms and snoop around. Maybe you borrow each other's clothes without asking. But have you ever heard of spying *animals*? The military has tried to make it happen!

In the 1960s, cats were trained by the CIA to spy on the Russians. The CIA is a US spy agency run by the government. First, the cats had surgery to have microphones put in their ears. Then, recording devices were placed underneath the cats' ribs. The idea was that the cats could record Russian secrets

Fact
Cats make great spies because of the way they walk: their back paws step nearly in the same place as their front paws did beforehand, which limits their tracks and makes less noise.

Cats are excellent trackers. This is why they make great spies!

Freeze! Drop Your Nuts!

In 2007, the Iranian army arrested fourteen squirrels for spying. The reason? The army claimed the rodents were wearing recording devices, but they were captured before they could do any real damage.

without being detected. The project was called Operation Acoustic Kitty.

Unfortunately, the mission did not work. The first cat on the job got run over by a car. Plus, cats are stubborn and hard to train. They will not do anything they do not want to do!

So far, the US military has not been able to successfully train any animal to actually be a spy. But scientists are trying to figure out a way to fit bees and wasps with devices just like the ones used in Operation Acoustic Kitty. The equipment would have a video camera and even a remote control. If their efforts work, experts believe these bugs could gather important information for the US military. They could even help solve hostage emergencies, when people are captured and held, usually for money.

Winged Warriors

If you have ever been to a public park, you probably know that pigeons love to coo and peck. But these birds are actually quite smart. They have two special talents. Pigeons can be trained to fly to a specific spot and back again. They can also navigate from one place to the next—and remember the route!

Fact
It usually takes about eight weeks to train a carrier pigeon to do its job.

During World Wars I and II, more than fifty-four thousand pigeons were used to deliver messages, maps, and other important papers between military units. The documents were put inside small tubes that were then attached to the birds' legs. Sometimes the birds carried the materials in larger sacks on their backs.

Pigeons have excellent eyesight. They have 360-degree vision!

Because of their impressive work, the birds were called carrier pigeons.

Carrier pigeons are fast. They can fly at speeds of up to sixty miles (ninety-seven kilometers) per hour! They can also travel for a long time without stopping. During World War II, carrier pigeons often flew an average of 400 miles (644 km) in one

Pigeons are still used to carry blood samples from remote areas of Britain and France.

The Bird, the Legend

History's most famous carrier pigeon was named Cher Ami. During World War II, the bird flew on twelve missions. He once saved two hundred soldiers from being killed after he delivered an important message at just the right time.

trip. Sometimes they even carried cameras that took photographs of enemy targets.

Many military veterans say they could not have done their jobs without the help of carrier pigeons. In fact, some of the birds even got awarded for their work. The most respected birds were given top honors for their brave military service. They were awarded the Distinguished Service Medal and the Purple Heart.

Sleek Swimmers

Dolphins, sea lions, and beluga whales are magnificent creatures. They are smooth. They are sleek—and boy, are they slippery!

Beginning in 1960, the US military started training underwater mammals to deliver important equipment to divers. They also taught them to find people lost at sea. Seven years later, the US Navy Marine Mammal Program took the job one step further. They taught sea lions, whales, and dolphins to find underwater explosives.

Psst. Pardon Me.

Dolphins are trained to guard harbors against enemy divers. If an enemy approaches, the dolphins bump a small device onto the diver's back. The device pulls the diver up to the surface, where he is captured.

Sea lions are helpful to the military because they are amphibious. They are comfortable on land and in water.

Like their relatives the killer whales, dolphins send out sound signals while they are swimming. The sound waves bounce off objects in the surrounding environment. This is called sonar. Dolphins can learn important information from the return echoes. They can create a mental map of where they are swimming and use it to navigate the area. This is called echolocation. Because of sonar and echolocation, dolphins are able to find mines in the water. They drop a weight next to each mine so navy divers can get rid of them.

Bottlenose dolphins are better than any machine at detecting mines.

Fact
Sea lions have special nerves in their whiskers to help them sense vibrations from food they want to eat or other objects in the water.

Unlike dolphins, sea lions do not use sonar. But they have above-average eyesight. Plus, they are naturally skilled divers. Some are even better than humans! Sea lions help the US Navy pick up lost equipment fired from ships. They also search for underwater explosives.

Military Mascot
Hall of Fame

From dogs to cats and honeybees to rats, lots of animals help people in the military be the best they can be. Some of the jobs, like diving for mines, are hard. But one of the easiest jobs in the military is the one Wojtek the bear had: being a friend!

Gruffy Goats

If you thought a bear was wild, goats are very popular military mascots. In fact, they are the proud leaders of armies in Spain, England, Wales, and even the United States. Bill the Goat is the mascot of the US Naval Academy!

Like everyone in life, soldiers need someone they can lean on and talk to during tough times. Someone—or some*thing*. Animals are lovable, dependable, and super cute. So what could be better than having a cuddly (and sometimes oily) pal around at all times to help you feel great?

It is time to meet some of the greatest animal friends in military history. Get ready to smile big. Welcome to the Military Mascot Hall of Fame!

Sir Nils Olav

Sir Nils Olav is a king penguin. He is the colonel in chief of

Sir Nils Olav lives in the Edinburgh Zoo. He greets Norwegian soldiers when they visit the Scottish capital.

Fact
The British army has nine official animal mascots, and each gets a rank, salary, and free food!

28

Quintas Rama is a Bengal tiger. He became a military mascot in 2012.

Norway's Kings Guard and wears a badge on his flipper. In August 2008, he was made a knight. Sir Nils Olav is the first penguin to receive this award in Norway.

Quintus Rama

A big, beautiful tiger named Quintus Rama is the mascot of the Royal Australian Regiment. He sleeps a lot and

Courage has served as a military mascot for almost thirty years!

weighs almost 440 pounds (200 kilograms)!

Courage

The Australian 2nd Cavalry Regiment has a wedge-tailed eagle named Courage as its mascot. Wedge-tailed eagles are the largest birds of prey in Australia.

Books

Calkhoven, Laurie. *Military Animals*. New York, NY: Scholastic, 2015.

Orr, Tamra B. *Animals Helping to Keep the Peace* (A True Book). New York, NY: Scholastic, 2015.

Patent, Dorothy Hinshaw. *Dogs on Duty: Soldiers' Best Friends on the Battlefield and Beyond*. New York, NY: Bloomsbury USA Children's, 2014.

Shotz, Jennifer Li. *Max: Best Friend. Hero. Marine*. New York, NY: HarperCollins, 2017.

Websites

ASPCA

https://www.aspca.org

The American Society for the Prevention of Cruelty to Animals is a national group that works to prevent cruelty to animals.

National Marine Mammal Foundation

http://www.nmmf.org/service.html

The foundation cares for and rehabilitates navy marine mammals and works to inform the public about the mammals' use in military practices.

US War Dogs Association

http://www.uswardogs.org

This group educates the public about military service dogs and establishes war dog memorials throughout the United States.

Published in 2019 by Enslow Publishing, LLC.
101 W. 23rd Street, Suite 240, New York, NY 10011

Copyright © 2019 by Enslow Publishing, LLC.

All rights reserved.

No part of this book may be reproduced by any means without the written permission of the publisher.

Library of Congress Cataloging-in-Publication Data
Names: Burling, Alexis, author.
Title: Animals in the military / Alexis Burling.
Description: New York : Enslow, [2019] | Series: Animals at work | Includes bibliographical references and index. | Audience: Grades 3-6.
Identifiers: LCCN 2017051696| ISBN 9780766096196 (library bound) | ISBN 9780766096202 (pbk.) | ISBN 9780766096219 (6 pack)
Subjects: LCSH: Animals—War use—Juvenile literature.
Classification: LCC UH87 .B87 2019 | DDC 355.4/24—dc23
LC record available at https://lccn.loc.gov/2017051696

Printed in the United States of America

To Our Readers: We have done our best to make sure all website addresses in this book were active and appropriate when we went to press. However, the author and the publisher have no control over and assume no liability for the material available on those websites or on any websites they may link to. Any comments or suggestions can be sent by e-mail to customerservice@enslow.com.

Photo Credits: Cover, p. 1 U.S. Navy photo by Photographers Mate 1st Class Brien Aho; p. 5 Martin Mecnarowski/Shutterstock.com; p. 7 U.S. Navy/Getty Images; p. 9 Michael Potter11/Shutterstock.com; p. 10 Stock Montage/Archive Photos/Getty Images; p. 13 © iStock/debibishop; p. 14 AFP/Getty Images; p. 16 Martin Ruegner/The Image Bank/Getty Images; p. 18 © iStock/CCeliaPhoto; p. 21 hrui/Shutterstock.com; p. 22 Gallinago_media/Shutterstock.com; p. 25 Willyam Bradberry/Shutterstock.com; p. 26 kansarin/Shutterstock.com; p. 28 Alexey Seafarer/Shutterstock.com; p. 29 CreativeMedia.org.uk/Shutterstock.com; p. 30 Seokhee Kim/Shutterstock.com.